AF264530

Other titles
by

Corey Hamilton

Keep Left
Society's Grip
Exit Is A Safe Place
No One Shall Be Spared
Open Up
Mash Notes: vol 2
Too Personal
Lonely Night Songs
2 Days
Unhyped
Time Marches On
Thirty Three
VI
What If?
Magic Bus
How I Remember It
Cease & Desist
Sensible Shoes
Do Not Ever Have Any Good Ideas
DNA
I Am NOT With The Band
Wedge Politics
My Side Project

Mash Notes

Library and Archives Canada Cataloguing in Publication

Hamilton, Coery, 1971-
    Mash notes / Corey Hamilton.

Poems and prose.
ISBN 978-0-9697305-5-2 (v. 1)

    I. Title.

PS8565.A5347M38 2008   C811'.54   C2007-906816-2

"Machine" © 1993 No Means No/Socan (ASCAP). Taken from the album "Why Do They Call Me Mr. Happy?" Lyrics used with permission.

Front cover photograph and photographs on pages 65 & 103 by Corey Hamilton © 2005. Author photograph on back cover by Mark Kozub © 2005. Design/Layout by Corey Hamilton

First Printing

Published by Dramatic Situations
          P.O. Box 696
          Edmonton, AB
          T5J 2L4
          CANADA
www.dramaticsituations.com

printed on 100% recycled paper.

Mash Notes

Corey Hamilton

F.Y.I.

The short story "MASH" was started in 1994 with Wayne originally being a psychology student, not a student of photography. Being as how I knew nothing about psychology and a lot about photography (I have a diploma in Photographic Technologies) I decided to change Wayne's studies. Subsequently I finished the short story in three days in 2005.

As for the poetry, I selected a number of pieces from as far back as my days in High School to 2005. I placed the pieces in numerical order so the reader can see how I progressed. Although some may say REgressed, (oh well). Regardless, I hope that you enjoy the ride. I know that I did!

Thanks.

None of the persons, places and events in the short story "MASH" are in any way real. Any relation to persons living or dead are purely coincidental.

The poetry in just the opposite.

masculine n 1 : a male person 2 : a noun, pronoun, adjective, or inflectional form or class of the masculine gender 3 : the masculine gender
mas·cu·lin·ize \'mas-kyə-lə-ˌnīz\ vt -ized; -iz·ing : to give a preponderantly masculine character to; esp : to cause (a female) to take on male characteristics
ma·ser \'mā-zər\ n [microwave amplification by stimulated emission of radiation] : a device that utilizes the natural oscillations of atoms or molecules between energy levels for generating electromagnetic radiation in the microwave region of the spectrum
1mash \'mash\ n [ME, fr. OE māx-; akin to MHG meisch mash] 1 : crushed malt or grain meal steeped and stirred in hot water to ferment (as for the production of beer or whiskey) 2 : a mixture of ground feeds for livestock 3 : a soft pulpy mass
2mash vt 1 a : to reduce to a soft pulpy state by beating or pressure b : CRUSH, SMASH <~ a finger> 2 : to subject (as crushed malt) to the action of water with heating and stirring in preparing wort
3mash vt [prob. fr. 2mash] : to flirt with or seek to gain the affection of
mash n : CRUSH 3
MASH abbr mobile army surgical hospital
1mash·er \'mash-ər\ n : one that mashes <a potato ~>
2masher n : a man who makes passes at women
1mask \'mask\ n [MF masque, fr. OIt maschera] 1 a (1) : a cover or partial cover for the face used for disguise (2) : a person wearing a mask : MASKER b (1) : a figure of a head worn on the stage in antiquity to identify the character and project the voice (2) : a grotesque false face worn at carnivals or in rituals c : an often grotesque carved head or face used as an ornament (as on a keystone) d : a sculptured face or a copy of a face made by means

OIt maschera] and often fanta gathering 2 : outward show
2masquerade : to go about : to assume th
mas·quer·ad·e
1mass \'mas\ n lit., dismissal at fem. of missus, : the liturgy of t Latin rite 2 of ~es held at thr ordinary of the
2mass n [ME m massein to knea gate of matter u : massive qualit vividness —F. <the great ~ of Sullivan> (4) property of a bo taken as a meas it to have weight and time constit physical measur number <a grea in a compact gr b : the body of pl. <a better futi

MASH

Wayne Crawford is a 28 year old photography student in his second year. He is attending a local University and lives in a large flat with his 32 year old girlfriend, Lindsey Warren. She is a dancer, and her career is about to take off. Lindsey finished school 2 years ago and now she is with a local dance troupe. The troupe has been getting international press for the last 5 years. Lindsey has been feeding herself via grants. If everything goes well she will be going to Japan next year with her troupe. This will be her first paying gig, and will be her first trip outside of North America.

Wayne has been subsisting on student loans and a part time job at a camera store. He has saved up enough money to go to Japan with Lindsey. He is a pack rat with books, records, cds, photographs and most of all money. So to save a few thousand dollars was a breeze. The trip will happen after he graduates. Just like Lindsey, Wayne dreams of conquering the world with his art.

Wayne's life is like a grandfather clock that never needs to be reset. Totally stable and complete, moving along like a well oiled machine.

This will all change in the second semester of his second year of school.

Ron is 37 years old, 5 foot 9 and has oily, sandy blonde hair. He always seems to have 4 day old stubble on his face and weighs about 240 pounds with a bit of a pot belly. He has blue/green eyes that look too normal, if that's possible. He looks like he is a robotic clone of someone you would see in a bad sixties science fiction movie. His dull eyes rarely blink and things just go screaming over his head, like red lights, no loitering, private property and what is right or wrong. He doesn't and won't flinch when he misses something. He used to, but now Ron is so used to missing things that it no longer bothers him. He is like that robotic clone from the sixties that has no emotions.

Ron's thoughts though are very jumbled up, so much so that he can barely contain them. He doesn't and won't flinch when a thought comes busting out of him loudly in the middle of a mall food court at peak hours. The only release Ron has is to pick his victims at random and hurt them with his tool. On the inside Ron is a very sick person. On the outside he is so normal, and again, if it is possible, too normal even if he has the looks of a derelict. He looks as if he wouldn't hurt a fly, but looks can be deceiving and that's what is frightening about Ron.

It is late August and Wayne is preparing his notes and such from last year so that he is not a total victim in year two, the final year, of Photography.

Wayne is working away diligently at his small desk. Most desks are small for him though because he is so tall and lanky. He is in the south corner of his and Lindsey's flat. In the western corner is Lindsey's stereo, weights and all of her other needs for her dancing. The kitchen is in the eastern corner, the bathroom the northern and living room is in the centre of the whole place with the "bedroom" in between the north and west corners.

None of these are actual "rooms" because there are no walls. They live in a fairly large flat, or loft, that takes up one whole floor (besides the door that leads to the stairs and elevator on the south/ eastern side of the flat. The walls have two windows, one wall panel, two windows and one wall panel, etc.. They have lots of light, with several plants. They will need attending soon.

Wayne brushes his long light brown hair out of his eyes and looks around. Everything is very open in their home, so they don't really need walls (except when company comes over). Wayne's blue eyes see the plants that need watering and he gets distracted (which he does easily and often). He gets up to water all of the plants in the rooms. The only indication of actual rooms is that they have large, delicately decorated rugs in the bedroom, living room and wayne's "office". Their home has a very simple layout. Simple and open, that's how the two of them like it, no complications, just smooth rides.

Lindsey is out buying groceries, it is her turn this weekend. Wayne will help her unload when she returns. There shouldn't be much to buy because it was his turn to go grocery hunting on wednesday. He finishes with the plants and goes back to his desk and finishes his note work

Wayne then gets up and approaches the living room, sits on the couch and turns on the television. The couch and the television are on an angle to the whole layout. They sit facing the east corner with the television facing the west. This is so as not to get too much light glaring off of the television, or blinding your eyes while you watch the t.v..

Wayne is fairly relaxed. It is 10:40 in the morning on this Saturday so he just sits there flipping channels back and forth. He and Lindsey are both early risers. This makes things less complicated. Their timetables work out so that they get to see each other often and problems like never seeing each other just doesn't occur. Wayne is just killing time by sitting and watching television. He's not really paying much attention, he is just flipping back and forth staring blankly at the screen watching all of the ads, news, info-mercials, etc. waiting for Lindsey to return.

Ron is not sick. Ron is not sick. Ron is not sick. Ron keeps saying this to himself over and over, again and again. Ron has his pruning shears, he is going to find his next victim. Ron is not sick. Ron is not sick. Ron is not sick.

Lindsey is back from grocery shopping now. It is around 1 pm. She was gone for about 3 hours, which is a little slow for her, but she was out dancing late last night so she doddled a bit.

"I'm back like a virus!" exclaims Lindsey. Lindsey has a very good sense of humour and that's one of the things Wayne likes about her. Wayne is too earnest for much of a sense of humour and he sometimes wonders what Lindsey sees in him. He is a bit of a stick in the mud sometimes but Lindsey doesn't seem to mind.

Wayne notices that Lindsey is wearing a new outfit and compliments her on it. She explains that not much was needed for groceries so she decided to treat herself before she went food shopping. The outfit is beige coveralls except there are no pant legs, just a dress that ends just above her knees. Lindsey wears a white sports bra and sandals, the whole thing looks extremely comfortable to Wayne. Wayne likes it because it shows off her well toned body, like her back, arms and legs. Wayne thinks her neck and back are her best attributes. Not to leave out her breasts and rear end which is firm from years of dancing.

They chat while putting the groceries away and when they finish they look out the kitchen window silently. Wayne stands behind Lindsey breathing into the side of her neck. Smelling her long black hair and skin he pushes aside her pony tail and notices that her head is looking up and her eyelids are almost closed on her light blue eyes. He moves his hands onto her ribs, just under her breasts and kisses her cheek. Wayne's hands are gently caressing her ribs and underside of her breasts. He is so gentle on Lindsey that it feels like a light breeze on her skin. He is following the ridges of her ribs because they are exposed.

Lindsey extends her arms out and places the palms of her hands on the window as she starts to breathe slightly heavier. She moves her body so it is now pressing against the window and her hands go behind her into Wayne's front pants pockets. She pulls him right against her back and now tries to undo his pants. He slowly removes one of the clasps on her "coveralls". All the while his left hand is still caressing her stomach, ribs and breasts.

Lindsey turns to face Wayne and they kiss each other slowly and passionately while undressing each other. Wayne is just wearing his shirt and boxers. Lindsey is wearing only her underwear as they move towards the bed.

Outside the day goes on trudging slowly towards the stark evening.

A very small and young Labradour retriever is barking furiously in its back yard. There is someone in the alley watching him but no one in the house believes it. The dog keeps on barking and finally the owner bellows at it to shut up. The dog lets out a sad little yip and stares at the one eye he sees between two fence boards. It doesn't like the smell of the human on the other side because he smells sick.

Even though it is August outside, it is not very hot, one can feel fall creeping in. It seems quite hot to Wayne and Lindsey though, for they have been making lover for the last hour and a half. The bed is so big that they can move around a lot.

"I can't remember my name. I can't remember my name. I can't remember my name," keeps on going through Wayne's head while Lindsey and him have sex. Eventually they both come. They lay silent while he remembers that he is "Wayne". They chat a little and then they go off to sleep.

"Yes, that's it, I am Wayne," Wayne says in his head.

Suddenly there is another smell but this one is nice. It smells like those crispy treats it gets at special times on special days. It moves closer and notices that the human is smiling and has put one of the treats just out of its reach. The young pup looks at the man and then the treat and can't resist. It sticks its nose then its left paw between the fence boards. Its paw comes close to the treat but the treat is suddenly jerked back. The puppy tries again with its left paw and has it!

As the pup slowly pulls the treat towards itself the man grabs the puppy's left paw and without warning there is a sharp snap, and the puppy starts howling. The pup no longer has a left paw. It is laying on the other side of the fence with the treat. Blood is spurting out onto the man's hand, the grass and the brown and white fur of the puppy.

Ron tosses the biscuit lightly to the puppy but the tiny dog isn't interested in treats anymore. Ron runs off because he hears the owner coming. Ron realises that again another puppy won't take Ron's treat after Ron has cropped the puppy. Ron pushes the realisation aside and hops on the nearest bus in the nick of time. All the while Ron repeats to himself, "Ron is not sick. Ron is not sick. Ron is not sick."

Wayne likes having sex but this is the first time ever that he initiated it. Usually Lindsey starts it all because Wayne is obsessively paranoid about <u>not</u> raping her.

Wayne likes having sex but this is the first time ever that he initiated it. Lindsey didn't seem to mind, but Wayne doesn't understand why it bothers him so much.

Wayne likes having sex but this is the first time ever that he initiated it.

School has started for Wayne.

Wayne and Lindsey's flat is on the southside and school the northside, so during peak hours it is an hour long ride. Lindsey is luckier. Her troupe practices a lot closer so she usually walks for the exercise. Wayne on the other hand day dreams his way to University in the morning with the radio turned off. In the afternoon the radio is turned on. It is his routine now. School has started so he has to get back into his routine. He likes the silence in the morning and the music in the afternoon.

Wayne is straight, "Never make any waves," his father told him when Wayne was a child of only 6. 2 years later his father was dead and it was junior high before Wayne understood what his father told him. Wayne's father was straight too, so his mother told Wayne, and from what Wayne remembered from when he was young he would agree with his mother. His father reminded him of the man on the front cover of that "Pink Floyd" album. The one with the two men shaking hands, the man on the right is on fire. "Wish You Were Here" he says aloud. Both men are in suits. Wayne's father reminds him of the man who wasn't on fire. Except that Wayne's father would never ever shake hands with someone like <u>that</u>. The band was trying to be smart with some sort of metaphor, like the man was shaking the hand of the devil or something. Again, Wayne's father wouldn't do that because he was a straight, good man, for that's what Wayne's mother told him. Now she is dead too. She died last year. Without telling Wayne what his father died from, he guesses that she never wanted to talk about it and Wayne didn't want to make waves.

Her death happened in his first year of University, part way through the second semester. Wayne is a bit of a loner so he has only two real friends, one being Lindsey and the other graduated last year from the Photography program and moved to the other side of the country. They said that "it" would be hard to deal with. They said that because of "it," his marks may drop and he may get easily distracted. Well none of "it" was true. In fact "it"made him more determined to do well in school. And he did do well in school. And, yes, he did get distracted, but then again wouldn't anyone?

Don't get Wayne wrong, he did cry and was upset for a little while but it didn't shatter his life. He had Lindsey after all and she was a pillar of strength for him. Wayne's mother's death wasn't totally unexpected though. First she had a bout of cervical cancer when Wayne was 16. The doctors said that she would be alright after her treatments. Four years later her mother found a lump on her left breast and they gave her 3 years to live because the cancer had progressed so far. She hung on for 7 years and then died. So it's not like Wayne didn't expect it.

Wayne's mother always made things seem like they would turn out okay. His mother reminded him of the "Mona Lisa". Some men he had met said that that painting just pissed them off. Wayne knew why. These type of men don't like seeing a confident woman. Well screw them because that is exactly why he liked the "Mona Lisa". She looked calm and confident and in control.

Just like Wayne's mother. His mother said things that would calm him down when he was upset. Like just before she died, she said that he would be alright and that they would be joined again as a family with father and Wayne. And that Wayne would take good care of himself because his mother had faith in him. That made Wayne feel calm, so when she died a few days later it wasn't as bad.

Wayne was an only child so he didn't have anyone to bring him down except himself. That would never happen because Wayne is straight.

At school Wayne's hard work in semester 1 and 2 pay off. Now he has just 4 courses in semester 3, and 2 in semester 4. Wayne took extra courses in year one because Lindsey and him already knew about the possibility of a paying show in Japan. Wayne wanted a lighter load in year two/semesters 3 and 4. He's taking Commercial/Industrial Photography, Colour Photography Techniques, Portraiture and Photothesis in semester 3. Semester 4: Colour Lab Techniques and Portfolio. This leaves him with more time to work at the camera store. Today is orientation and it will be life changing for Wayne, for he sees the new teacher that his "dysfunctional family" of classmates ("dysfuctional" because everyone is trying to get one up on the other & family because there are only 31 students, including himself.).

Back to the new teacher, she doesn't blend in well with the other instructors because she is dressed all business and the other three male teachers are dressed semi-casual. The "family" includes the second years and now the first year students. No one catches Wayne's eye in the first year, so he is mesmerised by the new teacher. He looks around and sees no one else staring at her or him. Everyone starts introductions, first the instructors, then the students.

All Wayne hears is, "blah blah blah," until the new female teacher pipes up with, "My name is Anne Wetteland and I will be your instructor for mostly first year courses with the exception of 2nd year Portfolio and Colour Lab Techniques." Then Wayne hears, "blah blah blah" from everyone else. He noticed that as she talked she looked everyone directly in the eye. Her stare gets to him and she mouthed something to him. No, she asked Wayne for his name because it was her turn and he was staring at her trying to see what sort of breasts she had underneath her suit jacket. Everyone is tittering.

"Uh...Wayne...Wayne...Crawford. Sorry. I am tired".

Anne smirks and says, "Well Wayne, try and wake up before the courses actually start tomorrow, because I am sure that I can speak for the other instructors when I say that we don't want to be your mother and have to wake you up every other morning."

More tittering while Wayne smiles sheepishly and looks down at his knees briefly. When the students start introducing themselves again Wayne looks back up at Anne.

Wayne has always been attracted to older, confident women. He figures that Anne is in her late thirties or early forties. Her arms are still crossed. He hopes that she will eventually break her statuesque stance and reveal a wedding ring or no wedding ring.

"I can't remember my name. I can't remember my name. I can't remember my name", Wayne repeats in his head over and over. Anne is wearing dress pants, dress shirt and a coat. The shirt is buttoned up to the second button from the top revealing her Adam's apple and the rest of her neck. Her skin is creamy white and Wayne wishes he could go up and rub the back of his hand gently on her neck in slow circles. Her clothes all match her hair's silvery/blonde colour. Anne's hair is cut like a little boy's would be cut and parted on the right side. Wayne estimates that she is about 5 foot 5 and is about 120 pounds. Her eyes are a shade of blue that is similar to the caps on those Bic pens that most students use. A medium shade of blue but very rich in colour. The colour of her eyes, the semi-high cheekbones, full lips the oval shape of her head all make her stare quite intense.

As everyone gets up to leave after a few more personal introductions with a few instructions from the instructors, everyone leaves.

Wayne notices that Anne is not wearing a wedding ring. He thinks to himself that semester two will be a good one.

A small miniature doberman was barking madly at the man behind the fence, but now it has stopped. The dog's head is cocked to the right side and it is watching the man crouching behind the fence on the gravel alley. It is watching very intently, for now it doesn't feel threatened very much on its side of the fence, in the grass, near its home and owners.

The man is reaching into his pocket now and the dog starts to growl quietly. The man has pulled a biscuit out of his pocket. The tiny doberman at first refuses to come near, but when the man places the treat underneath the fence it slowly gets up and moves towards the treat and man.

The man pulls the treat to his side of the fence and the dog realises that its nose is too big to fit under the fence, so the dog starts to bat at the treat until it is on the dog's side of the fence. Suddenly, the man reaches under and grabs its left paw and there is a loud snap. The dog experiences the most amount of pain it has ever felt in its life.

The dog's howling has attracted the attention of one of the owners but Ron's hand has gotten wedged underneath the fence boards. The dog hobbles over to the patio doors where the owner is. Now the owner is coming toward Ron, but his hand is still stuck. Ron is frantic now because the owner spots his dog and bellows, "What the fuck is going on out here?!" Just then Ron yanks his hand out from under the fence scraping multiple layers of skin off of his hand and takes off. All the owner sees is the back of a man running very quickly down the alley.

"I can't remember my name. I can't remember my name. I can't remember my name," Wayne thinks to himself as a new plan comes into his head. Wayne is thinking all of this up as he's driving to work from the University. He has the University station on the radio because it makes him feel different. This is because he likes the music that this one DJ plays on his show. It is an "alternative show" playing mostly independent Canadian music like D.O.A., Forbidden Dimension, Weakerthans, Rheostatics, Constantines, etc.. Just because Wayne hasn't heard of these bands and the music that they play, which makes him feel different, doesn't mean he isn't straight. Wayne will only listen to this music in the afternoon car rides and home alone. He respects Lindsey's choices because it is her lifeline to dance right now.

The DJ tells Wayne that the next band is called No Means No and the song is "Machine" from the album, "Why Do They Call Me Mr. Happy?" The song starts kind of quiet with just bass guitar and then a man's voice:

> *I don't like to see you cry*
> *You're alone and I know why*
> *I can free your life from sin*
> *Open up and let me in*
> *Let me in, let me in, let me in, come in*

Next the whole band starts. Wayne drives on to the methodical rhythm of the bass, drums, guitar and voice. Wayne must have a plan before he goes home from work tonight because this music makes him feel different. Different, like a machine that can't remember his name.

Ron is not sick. Ron is not sick. Ron is not sick. Ron is not...

It's 3 weeks later and Wayne has bought the cd by No Means No and he is glad he did because he feels rebellious listening to some of the songs on the album. It is so different from what he is used to. Fuck Pink Floyd! As usual he skips to his favourite song on it, the one he heard on the radio called "Machine". He starts humming along with the catchy song:

> *Machine, I'm a good machine*
> *Machine I'm a good machine*
> *On you I lean, I lean, I lean, I lean, on you I lean*
> *Machine, I'm a good machine*

Wayne has just read the lyric sheet, he feels as if he knew all of the lines already. "The Land Of The Living", "The River", "I Need You Now" and of course the funniest tracks, "Kill Everyone Now" and "Cats, Sex and Nazis".

> *Believe in one another*
> *Depend on one another*
> *I am the other*
> *I'm a good machine*
> *Machine, I'm a good machine*

"Machine" is such a good song but he figures that he will like the rest of the cd even more in the final days of his plan. Which should work out by the end of the second semester. For now he had better give it a rest for if Lindsey sees/hears him listening to something like this she would probably think that there is something wrong with him. Even though she dances in an "alternative troupe" No Means No would be too alternative, if that's possible.

Wayne is well along into the first semester and the next assignment is "Illustrative/Editorial Table Top" which should be a breeze. Coast, coasting. Coast, coasting. ASK. Plan, planning. Plan, planned? Planned. Wayne is straight? Wayne is straight. Just do the jewellry assignment that is due in 2 weeks and coast some more.

After class Wayne decides to relax from his hard week by going for lunch in "The Atrium" on the campus. Watch the news, eat, listen to his discman that he recently bought which has the No Means No cd in it. The cd hasn't left his discman except to go into his car or home stereo.

At "The Atrium" Wayne is disturbed by the news report of somebody brutally crippling dogs at random. Wayne can't eat anymore, he puts on his discman and will go and do the new assignment and business report as well and blah blah blah.

Ron never cleans his tool off after he has done his job. He feels that it is the same thing that hockey players do in the playoffs, not shaving until the season is over. Ron also heard that one goalie even talked to his goal posts. Ron doesn't talk to his tool because that is stupid because it won't talk back.

Back to the task at hand. Ron has been trying to get the attention of a small shitzu while he was thinking about hockey and stuff. Ron has been making faces, squashing his face in between the fence boards and spitting, but all the dog has done is sit there on the steps of the porch looking at Ron with mild contempt.

Ron is getting very angry. Finally Ron gives the dog the raspberry, sending spit and snot(that was running from Ron's nose) flying. This has finally gotten the dog's interest. Ron places a biscuit down in anticipation, but before Ron can react, the dog trots up, grasps the treat in its mouth and turns back to the porch,. promptly sitting down and devouring the treat.

Ron is furious. He starts placing a few more biscuits down a little farther away from the dog so it has to reach for them. The shitzu slowly trots over and when seeing that it can't reach the biscuits with its mouth, it turns around and begins to bury the biscuits in dirt, snow and gravel with its hind legs.

Ron blows a fuse. He reaches under the fence and grabs the dog's right hind leg and tries to slap the dog with his free hand. The shitzu is mildly irritated by this silly person and it turns and bites the hand that is grasping its leg. Ron finally comes to his senses, grabs his tool, yanks the dog close to him and without hesitation snips off the dogs left paw.

The dog lets out a shrill yelp and glares at the man for he has his eyes closed and is yelling at it as well as spitting.

Ron is yelling, "That will teach you! You stupid fuck head dog!" Ron then feels something warm and wet on his face. Ron opens his eyes to see that the shitzu is urinating in ron's eyes, mouth and face.

Ron is shocked and can't believe this is happening. Ron would do more damage but by this time he has to regain his senses because the dog's whining and Ron's yelling have all attracted the attention of the people inside house. They are super pissed it seems to Ron.

Ron runs away in the nick of time, and while he is running away he wipes the mixture of his and the dog's blood off of his hand on the back of his pants. Ron places his tool back in his pocket and with his "unbitt" hand wipes the dog urine off of his face mumbling to himself, "This is much harder than Ron expected."

It's Christmas break for Wayne and he can hardly wait to get Anne as a teacher next semester. Everything else in his life is on cruise control. He is in a mall trying to get regular as well as Christmas shopping done, but getting through all of the people and noise and action and more people puts him under some considerable pressure. His average marks were one thing, but right now he feels as if he is allergic to people. This thing he may have for Anne is getting him in a way he never expected. He feels as if everything is startling him. Anne, Lindsey, the dog butcher and even the lousy weather.

Wayne turns on his discman with the great No Means No cd in it, it is so good. He has been listening to it a lot in any cd player that is near him in public or not. Lindsey still hasn't heard it or Wayne's plan yet but that's okay. Wayne pushes his shopping cart around and zones out until a part in his favourite song, "Machine" starts up. The lyrics are striking a chord deep in his brain and he is not sure why.

I love it, believe me, you know it's true
Believe me, I know it, you'll love it too
I mean it, I see it, I know it's true
I see it, I know it, you'll love it too

When we walk and talk about it
Talk together I feel fine
When we walk and talk about it
Talk together, walk in line
We walk together, talk about it
Talk together, I feel fine
We talk about it, walk together
Talk together, walk in line
I guess I'm alright
Oh, yeh alright alright
You know I'm ok
Ok, alright, alright
Oh, yeh it's alright
Alright alright alright
I'm ok, it's alright, I feel fine, it's ok, it's alright, in fact it's fine

The lyrics are striking a chord deep in his mind and Wayne is not sure why. Wayne finishes his shopping and gets ready to leave thinking, "Everything is done here and I am alright, in fact I am fine. I am straight. I am straight?"

Ron doesn't feel like doing it today.

But he will anyway.

Ron will have to watch it because in the past when he feels this way he gets careless and makes mistakes.

"Hey look," Ron says to himself quietly, "there's another fucking poodle."

Ron hates poodles because they remind him of pakis or east

indians or whatever you want to call them. Both pakis and poodles yap loudly in their own language and can't back it up with anything. He knows, because Ron has seen everything, well almost everything. That doesn't matter because the poodle has spotted Ron and has started its fucking yapping.

Ron enjoys hurting poodles. Sometimes he lets the poodles bite his hand and then he would do his job. He stopped that awhile ago because he read that all poodles have rabies. Ron is willing to bet that pakis have rabies too. So he won't let poodles or pakis bleed on him. If he sees a bleeding paki that is.

Ron throws the biscuit down.

Ron's victim goes down on the biscuit.

Ron goes down on his victim.

Ron's victim goes down howling.

Ron goes down the alley as fast as his stocky legs can take him. Ron is not sick. Ron is not sick?

It is now 2 weeks into semester 2, year 2 and Wayne is still straight and still in cruise control. He will <u>try</u> and stay interested in his classes. Everything is fine. Wayne wishes all these dreams and thoughts and thoughts of dreams would all stop because everything is alright. Where is his discman with his damn No Means No cd? Just put those things in his ears and fade out for awhile.

I'm a big machine
yeh, yeh, yeh
Machine I'm a good machine
Of thee I sing, I sing, I sing of thee I sing
Machine, I'm a good machine

Believe in one another
Depend on one another
Be good to one another
I am the other
I'm a good machine
Yeh, yeh, yeh

"Ok, ok, ok, alright. Enough of this. Everything is fine. Forget your dead parents and the cross processing assignment and Lindsey and Anne. And Anne?" Wayne thinks to himself, almost waking Lindsey. It is time for him to get the shopping done while Lindsey sleeps in.

Anne's office door is open but Wayne knocks quietly anyway. Anne says to come in and Wayne does, his plan is going along smoothly.

"Here's the cross processing assignment. I wanted to give it to you personally because it is nearly late," Wayne speaks meekly

"Thanks Wayne, but I noticed that your marks went up in semester 2, year 1 and now they have been slowly declining. I don't beat around the bush, I am concerned," states Anne, all business.

"I will pick it up on Portfolio," mutters Wayne, but thinking this is a wrench. He then blurts out, "Maybe we could go to the Atrium and discuss this further?"

Anne quickly responds, "I don't feel that that is very professional Wayne, but if you do 'pick it up on Portfolio' then I won't need to worry, now will I?"

"No," mumbles Wayne, "Thank you."

"Bitch," thinks Wayne and leaves quickly as he came. "One unsuccessful plan....need a new one."

It is at this point that Wayne no longer really hears anything anyone else says, except for his discman. It is all just being transferred into second hand information. Everything gets distorted by his emotions (or lack thereof). He can only hear what he says, for everyone else's words are secondary. Wayne can't remember the last time he had made love to Lindsey and that's why he asked Anne out. Part of the plan that failed. He was hoping...seduce...seduction are bad words to Wayne, but he was hoping for something like that. Now there is going to be a change of plans and Wayne know what he has to do.

Listen.

Listen some more...

I love it, I made it, it's what I do
You know it, you've seen it, it looks like you

Wayne has to stop torturing himself about everything, he thinks to himself as the discman blares on:

Wayne hurries up and tears his headphones off of his head. He has to get out of this stuffy University. Away from anything that reminds him of his life with Anne and the school. He rushes out of the University like someone who is late for their subway train.

Ron is not sick. Ron is not sick. Ron is not sick. Ron keeps saying this to himself over and over, again and again. Ron has got his small pruning shears and is going to find his next victim.

Wayne is straight. Wayne is straight. Wayne is straight. Wayne keeps on saying this to himself over and over, again and again. Wayne now knows what he has to do. Wayne has to get to a hardware store A.S.A.P. and then back to the University.

Anne Wetteland is grading the last photograph, for her, forever, when Wayne walks into her office quietly. Just as Anne senses something she is struck on the back of her head until she is unconscious.

Wayne used the handles of a large set of pruning shear. Wayne gently kisses her forehead as he calmly lifts up her left arm.

A very tiny grey tea cup poodle is yapping like it was actually 60 times its size. It believes that it can scare the man hiding in the shadows of the garbage cans. He is watching the dog intently from the other side of the chain link fence.

The small poodle yaps like this so much that the owners are used to it and pay no attention from inside their home. So the dog continues unhindered. It continues yapping even as it sees three fingers holding a biscuit come through one of the diamond shaped holes in the fence. The dog recognises what the man is holding as a treat and decides that it wants it.

The poodle bounces over to the man like it bounced right out of a Bugs Bunny cartoon that Ron saw as a child. To Ron the dog's mouth is watering for the treat so much that it appears to be crazy with rabies.

For the first time Ron is still holding the biscuit when his victim snatches it. Ron simultaneously releases the biscuit with his left hand and grabs the poodle's left paw with his right hand. As Ron reaches for his tool, the poodles starts to panic and Ron drops his tool and his right hand gets stuck under the fence. The dog can't understand what's going on and before Ron can finish what he started the poodle lashes out at the stuck hand, which is still holding it's paw. The dog is a puppy so its teeth are razor sharp and cut through the exposed flesh on the underside of Ron's wrist. The dog continues biting and tearing until two streams of blood spew all over the gravel, new grass and other more springish items. Not to mention blinding the dog's eyes.

By this time Ron feels faint and releases the dog and is able to jerk loose his hand from the fence. The poodle bounces back 3 or 4 feet so he is well out of reach of Ron and his tool. The poodle is now bouncing again with blood soaked deep into its tight grey curls of hair around its mouth, eyes and fore paws. They are all red with Ron's blood. To Ron it seems as if the dog is acting triumphant with its barking and the way it hops forward a few steps and then back and then forth and then back again. All the while it watches Ron sitting on his ass with his legs spread out and his hands between them. Left hand has Ron's tool, his right hand nothing but blood. The blood is coming out slowly now but there is still a small puddle of blood between his legs.

Ron pokes at his right wrist with his pruning shears and the blood comes out more quickly. At this point in time Ron feels he is going to get in trouble and says aloud to himself, but looking at the poodle barking, "Ron must leave now." As he gets up he realises that he can't hear anything anymore. Ron stumbles off down the alley in a haphazard fashion.

Wayne is tired. Very tired. He has made his life so complicated. If he was unhappy with Lindsey he should have told her so.

Wayne is extremely glad that he decided against driving his car back to the University for now he can walk home and get straight with his machine plan. Wayne and Lindsey's home is on the southside, not exactly central because it is just south of downtown. So he has to walk through the mass rush of downtown at peak hours. The University is on the north side, so it is quite a long walk.

Wayne walks downtown regularly for groceries, to mail stuff, etc. so he is used to people moving about. Wayne is so engrossed in his thoughts that he plows into a man. Wayne is used to downtown freaks but this guy takes the cake. He smells funny, his hair is greasy, his face has stubble and is white. Judging by the look in the man's eyes, he is on a field trip to Jupiter.

Wayne apologises to the man and the man flinches at the same time that Wayne says sorry. The man replies half in a mumble, "Get home right away", and stumbles off. Wayne shakes his head and continues on his way.

If Wayne wasn't so self absorbed and looked away from the man's face he would have noticed that the man was holding his belly and that the bottom of his shirt, along with the top of his pants, were deep red with blood.

Wayne has more important things to worry about.

Ron is tired, very tired. He has made his life so complicated. That fucking poodle! Ron knew he should have made his pass at the chihuahua 10 blocks south. Maybe pakis can back their yapping up if a fucking poodle can. Ron knows that if he had gone after the chihuauau that he wouldn't be feeling so sick right now.

Ron stops dead in his tracks. Ron is downtown! Ron never goes downtown! Ron also realises that he has lost his tool! Ron is such a stupid head! Ron is such a stupid head! Ron is very frightened because he is downtown and he doesn't have his tool. Ron doesn't know what he will do now. It is at this point that Ron is jarred out of his stupor by one of the staring people. Ron looks up almost as if he is going to ask the man, "Why did you have to come along and stare at me?" The staring man apologises and Ron jumps. The people who stare have never, ever said anything to Ron. Ron is now even more scared, so he looks away from the starring man and mumbles, "Get home right away", as Ron skulks away.

Ron hates the staring people because, like the one who just spoke to him, they all hate him and Ron doesn't know why. They all look at him as if he is strange and wish that Ron would go away. That is why Ron hates the staring people. If Ron had his tool he would show the staring people a thing or two. He would take one of them, actually he would take the one who talked to him and gouge out his eyes with his tool. Then Ron would throw his useless staring people body at the rest of the staring people and laugh at them. Then Ron would yell at all of them, "You see, that's what happens to people who stare! You fucking stupid heads! You see! Didn't your stupid head moms teach you not to stare! Because that's what happens to people who stare!"

Ron snaps his fingers on his good hand and runs down the downtown alleys to avoid the starring people. Now Ron has a smile on his face.

A female janitor at the University is sweeping the halls and gets to the Photography Instructor's offices. One door is open slightly, so she knocks lightly. It is around 6:30 pm so it wouldn't be the first time that she found a teacher asleep at their desk. There is no answer so the janitor opens the door saying hello tentatively. The sight of a severed hand on a desk and blood all over a female is too much for the the janitor to comprehend. She lets out the loudest and longest scream she has in her whole life.

Wayne has been home for just fifteen minutes when his thoughts start getting jumbled up. He turns out the lights, puts his discman on and starts to realise what he has gotten himself into.

Wayne feels that his relationship with Lindsey was like his life was hidden underneath several dirty towels on their bathroom floor, when he first saw Anne. Anne was to be his saviour, but she wasn't and his mother wasn't around to calm him down.

Wayne has yet to realise that he is the one who put all of the restrictions on himself, not Lindsey, not Anne, not his parents, but it was himself. He is the one who made his life so mediocre. When Wayne starts to panic is when he comes to this realisation that everything he did or will do or were are totally under his control.

That's when Wayne starts to really panic. Even "Machine" can't save him now because he is being blown out of his complacency. His panic breaks him down and shoots him right out of the womb that he had made for himself. This womb had protected him from all of the damage that the world had caused him as well as he caused the world.

Wayne thinks about this book that he had read once, where the author said that we are all selfish in one way or another, whether we admit it or not. Wayne didn't believe it then, but he does now.

Wayne sits in the darkness of his kitchen and turns up his discman to the maximum and sits there listening to No Means No for the last time.

Lindsey is walking home and notices that their car is in their stall. Wayne, the introvert of late, should be at work. Lindsey goes over to the car and sits on the hood and dials the camera store up on her cell phone. When she asks for Wayne the man on the other end informs Lindsey that Wayne hasn't worked there in almost 5 months. Lindsey hangs up.

Lindsey has a sinking feeling as she approaches the front door with their upper level loft in it.

Ron is sitting down in a quiet, secluded alley near the University. Ron is sitting because he feels dopey. Ron has been dancing because he knows exactly what he will do after he has had a little nap. Ron will go find his tool, then Ron will go find the staring, talking man and gouge out his stupid head eyeballs. Then Ron will show them to the staring, talking man and laugh at him. Laughing, Ron will say, "Now you can't stare at me you big stupid head!" Then Ron will put the eyeballs into the staring, talking stupid head's mouth and say, "There, now you can't talk either you fucking stupid head!" Ron giggles to himself at how smart he is.

Ron feels very tired. Ron looks at his right wrist as he starts to lay down on his left side. Ron adjusts his coat underneath his head, as his eyes stay fixed on his right wrist. Ron is very comfortable now because he is ready for his nap. Ron needs a nap now because Ron is very sleepy.

Ron's right wrist is all crusty with tiny pieces of dirt, dog hair, his own flesh and of course his own blood. The bleeding stopped awhile ago but Ron pokes at it and blood starts to ooze slowly out of the one major wound. There are about 12 cuts total. One major gash, two others that are serious enough to warrant stitches and the rest are cuts and scratches and such.

Ron sure did have a number done on his hand. Ron feels it will be alright after he takes a nap. His hand will stop bleeding for good. Then Ron will be able to move it. Ron moves his right hand around and blood comes out slowly of the major wounds like little streams.

Ron puts his wrist on his belly and snaps his fingers with the other hand and giggles to himself, for when Ron wakes up he is going to show all of the staring people who is the boss once and for all. Ron snaps his fingers once more and goes into a deep sleep, dreaming that he hears sirens coming for him.

Lindsey enters the dark loft and hears a hissing sound. She quickly turns on the lights and is startled to see Wayne sitting at the kitchen table with his head phones on, which are making the hissing sound because they are blaring away. Wayne is staring at her and to Lindsey he looks like a cadaver.

Lindsey walks slowly into the kitchen while Wayne turns off his discman. Lindsey asks what's wrong and Wayne without removing his head phones, speaks quietly, "I love you but it is much too late for me now." Before Lindsey can ask what Wayne is talking about he smashes his discman three times against her head, knocking her off balance so that she falls and cracks her head against the stove.

Wayne takes the head phones off and drops them and the remnants of his discman and No Means No cd to the floor. He removes a magnet holding the 2 tickets to Japan and bends down and kisses Lindsey on the lips. Wayne then steps over her unconscious body and leaves. Locking up he thinks he should be able to squeeze the airline enough that they'll change the flight date to tomorrow or even later tonight.

By the time Lindsey wakes up 4 days later with her bloody, head achy head it is far too late to help Wayne.

There are several people playing and resting on this one beach on Okinawa, Japan.

A small boy is building a sand castle around himself when a hand breaks through an outer wall. At first the boy is annoyed that someone would be so rude as to ruin his fun. The boy gets up and notices that the person who stuck his hand through the wall of his magnificent castle is laying face down half in the water, half on the beach. The person is a man and everytime a wave rushes over the body it jerks the body a little farther into the boy's castle.

The young child cries out to his parents and they rush over to their sun to see a white man wearing only boxer shorts lying face down in front of their son. The husband and wife roll the man over only to realise that the tall, brown haired man is quite dead.

THE END

This short story was written
on two seperate occasions:
the first was: Jan. 6, 7, 8 in 1994
the second was: Jan. 26, 27, 28 in 2005
Sorry it took so long,
I'll try better next time.

THE SCOWL

The scowl is what I wear
It corrodes the outsides
It corrodes the insides

"Why don't you smile?"
People ask me
The reason is,
I have nothing to smile about

"Bull shit!" people say
But tell me
Do you really know
Anything about me?

You don't know why
I shouldn't smile or
Why I should smile

You could give me
One thing that would make me smile
Which is
Bravery.

NO FEELINGS

At times
I wish that I had
No feelings
Because time
After time again
I feel something
For the people I see
And
Then
They
Get
Shattered.

To make sure
Something like
This doesn't happen
Again
I'm loud
To cover my
Isolation
And I fear
It will last
Forever

some of this piece are quotes from the "MAGE" comic series.

GRATEFUL

Everyday
I take my senses
For granted
Senses
Sight
Hearing
Smelling
Taste and
Touch
And my mind,
Is "perfect"

I don't show it
But, yes
I am grateful
For them

I can see the sights of the world

I can hear the sounds of the world

I can smell the smells of the world

I can taste the tastes of the world

And I can feel the feelings of the world

And yes,
I am grateful

WHAT'S THE USE

I try and try,
But I can't seem
To get it through
My fat head

The school work
I can't understand
The art works
That don't satisfy
The life
That's unfulfilling

There is no point
In going on
When nothing
I do comes out right

There is no point.

this piece was written on
november 19, 1987 at 10:35 am
in sherwood park, ab

FIRST SNOW FALL

The snow is newly white
When the sun comes up
The reflection is so bright

Smell the fresh and crisp snow
And look at the picturesque scene
Of a mother deer and her doe

These are the mornings people wait for
So inhale deep and remember these
And after, never close your mind's door

GOING

He is going
And you feel responsible
You should

He is going
And you think you care
You don't

Oh, but you do
Oh, but you will
And then
You won't

He wanted to talk
And you didn't
He tried to talk
But you didn't

That is what he didn't like
Because it makes you...
It makes you feel useless

Now when you know something you'll act...
You will act strange to him
He probably doesn't like that

I think
And I believe
I know how he feels
Now that he is going (maybe)
I truly hope
That he will stay

SORE THUMB

I have this habit
I watch people in my classes
They don't watch me
I don't know why

There's the preps, the jocks, etc.
Some say I stand out
I think not
There's "little" people who do that for me

One guy in my class
Has average looks
Has average clothes
He seems so, average

And yet,
He stands out,
He is really different
I am not sure about him

He almost frightens me
I don't understand why,
But he does
I almost envy him

ARE YOU?

When you are young
You think you are younger
And wish you were older

When you are old
You think you are older
And wish you were younger

Wouldn't it be nice
To throw away the masks
And be able to be yourself?

BURNBURN
BURNBURN
BURNBURN
BURNBURN
BURNBURN
BURNBURNBURNBURNBURNBURN
BURNBURNBURNBURNBURNBURN
BURNBURNBURNBURNBURNBURN
BURNBURNBURNBURNBURNBURN
BURNBURN
BURNBURN
BURNBURN
BURNBURN
BURNBURN
BURNBURN
BURNBURN
BURNBURN
BURNBURN
BURNBURN
BURNBURN

CAVE IN

Thrust, push, pull, hit
I'm in such violence
Reflections of past
Present and future
Unnervingly present themselves
Upon me forcefully
Engraving their virus on me

On me
Please not on me
No, I am so helpless
Thrust, push, pull, hit
No more violence

Subconscious plays on me
And in me slowly
No love anymore
Just hate and bitterness
No more happiness
It becomes sadness
And no more will to live

On me
Don't drive on me
Leave me be
I'm pleasant, oh so pleasant
Don't make me hurt

I hurt too much
Thrust, push, pull, hit
Enough pain as it is
No more violence
Our father, who art in heaven
Hallowed be thy name

BOTTOM LINE

I've come from a place
You've never seen
I've come from a place
You've never been
I've come from a place
You simply abhor
I've come from a place
You've never heard of before

Time in, time out
It's up to you again
Time in, time out
I'll leave it up to you again

The wires can cross
And connect as one
The wires can cross
And work as one
The wires can cross
So as to see eye to eye
The wires can cross
So we can work to get by

Time in, time out
You'll look away
Time in, time out
You're afraid of your life everyday

Time in, time out
You're afraid of my life
So you won't play

PLAYED THE GAME

I am nothing but
Nothing
But you insist on
Attacking
Me with your smiles
And your past
I never was in
Your past
I apologize
But that's not
Good enough
For you
So your smiles
And smiley teeth
Past
Will bite me
For your knowledge
For your fun
Or your entertainment
Or your game
Of which I am not
A part of
But I am
A part of
By being near you
By looking at you
By looking in you
I became a part of
Your game
The final solution
Mean
Mean solution
Means
That I am nothing
Like you
And everything
Out you
For you are nothing but

Nothing
and I am nothing but
Nothing

YOU'RE TELLING ME

Don't call me
Anything like
That
You're telling me
I'm crazy
I don't like
It when
People tell me
Telling me
I'm something
But not it
I can call myself
A lot of things
But I call it
Telling me
You're telling me
I'm all alone
A loner
All alone
Don't call me that
Because you're not
You're just telling me
You're telling me
People telling me
Something
That's not true

SCHOOL BOSS

I'm writing
And in he
Catches comes
"Got nothing to do"
Got lots to do
"Get on it man"
And boss man
Turns reddy
Like he was
Embarrassed
To find me
To catch me
To see me
Doing "nothing"
What?
If you can't
Take giving shit
You shouldn't
Be in control
Be in control
Of taking shit
Too
Can you take
All of the above?
If not
Get the fuck out
Of your head office

INFLUENTIAL INTENTIONS

The day before I die
I want you to know one thing
I never understood influences
And their effects on me and others
My intentions were never to
Influence anyone
I just want to state my opinion
My intentions were never to be
Influenced by anyone
I just wanted to
Do my own thing

BEHOLDER OF THE EYE

The business man
Looked like
He was in a
State of shock
As he drove
By in his jeep
Such an elaborate
Image when
Seen through
A fish bowl
Imagine his
Facial matte
Is about the
Same as the
One you wear
When you gaze
Out of the bowl

WASTE

Women and men
Abusing and then excusing
A tight knit group
Causes inbreeding
Causes internal bleeding
That's why I left early
With my concrete moves
And through stop traffic
Never stopped me
Because your concrete
Never moves at all
I always move
Move on and up
While just painting
Watery nothings
Almost normal
But normally almost
Fucked up
Just another day
Of your week
To waste on me

TROLLEY

Back and forth
Question out of nowhere
Something about
Devotion reminds
Me of moist soil
Packed lightly
On a face
Back and forth
Except my life
Except my life
Self defecating
Accept my life
Accept my life
Back and forth
I'm going on
In no time
I'm going on
Without a flag
Without a meal
I need rest
From myself
Back and forth
Back and forth
Back and forth

GROUNDS

I hate the ground you walk on
I can feel it coming
Like when you are going to be sick
I'm going to make a mistake
(As usual) and you'll use it
To knock me away from
My only friend and lover
I've ever had and
I will only make it worse
I think you know this
That's why I don't want
To be around you at all
So if I make my mistake
You can't jump on me
I wish I could be around you
Make you grounded
So this won't happen
But it will
And when it does
I will die
On your grounds

CHATTEL

My tunnel vision
At a show
Hasn't put me
In a pawn shop's
Window just yet
I guess it could happen
If my aim
Is just a little off
But my aim
Hasn't been thrown off
Just yet
What do you know
You haven't seen me
In ages
You haven't even
Seen my age
What am I writing about?
What are you writing about?
Death is not a tragedy
It's the loss that's
The tragedy
Earth
Justice
And chaos
Is what I am
You are a method
With no rhyme nor reason
I'm not just
Reading between the lines
I am reading through
You weak lines

ALIENIST

Every time I think of you
I smell freshly cut lumber
And I see a shadow of you
Pulling up your pants
And leaving things in your oven
And other's ovens too
The only thing that
Is better than the real thing
Is your expectations of
Your healing methods on me
Something in a nut
Is that what you think
When I say that
I've never kissed a black woman
And I would really like to
And I've always wanted to
What would you say about that?
To tell you the truth
I don't really care
Maybe my back turning to you
Is from the pills you give me
Don't worry
This will be a short one
Because you're not worth
Any sort of length at all

DESIRES AND DEADLINES

Yes
This is a next year land
And I want to be able to
Say that I am satisfied
With where I'm at
Remember when you
Laughed about all the rain
Well you still do
Just now
It's that you realize that
The laughter hurts
Yes
And this is your neck
You want someone
Who can be a hero
Every minute
Of every day of the year
I'm not putting
My life in a freezer
Just for you
Or anyone else
Preparation
Execution
Follow up
Diagnostic
Exact science
No
I don't care if
You have the
Most letters
After your name
Or in it
I'm tired
And worn out
From hoping
That you'll figure it out
Before
I get it in the left ear

I'm tired
And worn out
I thought it was raining
But it never was
It was just the wind
It was just the wind

MNEMONIC

I wanted you to be with me
Tonight
I wanted her to be with me
Last night
It all starts with a kiss
And even angels lose their wings
Jesus
My words headed north
I don't know what to do or say anymore
I'd like to say that
I love you
But I don't think you'd believe me
I wanted you to be with me
Last night
When someone pointed out
That my special day was over
The stairs I've climbed
Weren't worth the stress and
The only words I thought of
When someone pointed out
That my special day was over
Were, thank you very much
And if you entered the room with me
Would the appropriate
Line of conjectures be
Just be friends
The things I think you're bruising
Are on me
Man over board!
Man over board!
My illusions, fantasies, dreams
Have pushed me over
And whenever I hear
"I wanna be adored"
By the Stone Roses
I think of slow dancing with you
And then us slipping into bed together
But I never learned how to dance slowly

And my special day was over long ago
And now it's time for
My own particular brand of
Cynicism and realism
That says it won't happen
Or that I don't have the time for it
Or that's too intense
Or that I'm too intense
But I'm not sure if
All of the above falls under
Cynicism and realism
Or pessimism
I don't know what to do anymore
I want you to hold me
Because I'm tired of trying to climb up
All of the time and
I believe it's time to lay down
For a little while
Lay down and heal from the wounds
Heal from the wounds
That your image did to me
Because I forced your image to hurt me
Behind your back
Without knowing
I'm tired and need to lay down
And heal from these self inflicted wounds

WRONG DIRECTION

Punk's not dead
It's in suspended animation and
Animation is the operative word
Come join the chant
Of this red neck zombie parade
With side trailing and hustling and all
Everything looks so nice and simple
When it's on the grey screen
I just wrote this to get it
Out of the way
I wrote this all from pieces
Of what I heard, saw and felt
But there's nothing like
A perfect addiction
There's nothing like
A pure addiction
One to bring you down
First paragraph
Of another paragraph
Keep on writing out
Everything I come in contact with
People say it's a waste of ink and paper
Explain your paper
I have one
Do you?
It's not an important sentence
It's my controlling idea
It controls me
And all of my perceptions
Industry requires
Who cares?
I only care of what
Common sense requires
It's my new way of writing
It's my new hand writing
I am walking along in a forest
And see that the trees
No longer have their natural color

They have turned into steel
The sky looks like
A tangle of circuits and wires
And I am feeling small again
This all has two meanings
And I think I forgot them both

TIER ONE

If I lost something
In a dream
Then it's really
A nightmare and
I don't want
To remember it
I've lost enough as it is
I don't need to
Dream about losing
More of myself
More of myself
Waking in the wind and
Walking in the wind
I'll keep walking
For as long as it takes
Because a failure is a quitter
Not someone who keeps trying
I'll keep on going
But don't ask me the score
Because usually when
I'm in a game
I don't keep score
Because it kills all of the fun
And what's achievement without fun?
It's like putting a message
On a carrier pigeon
And then locking the pigeon in a cage
Don't ask me the score
Because I don't know
Have you made up your mind
Because you've made up mine
If attitudes are infectious
Then yours isn't worth inhaling
And it doesn't warrant
Me getting near to you
And this is the last time
I'll write about someone like you
The last time I write about your name

The last time I write about your name
It probably never mattered
Because you probably never listened
I'm going to my recordings at home
Because this one's done

SNIPER

I was giving up
The expectation
Of being a student
And I will
Do unto others
As they have
Done to me
Sounds pretty good to me
Before I go
I won't come around
So don't expect
Anything from me
Before I go
While I'm still here
Don't look up to me
Look up to yourself
You shouldn't
Have to look up to anyone
But yourself
This game has gotten out of hand
Good hand gotten out of hand
When her one foot in the door
Gets hacked off
And I'm always wishing
That some one person or group
Will come into my place of work
And shoot it up
For something
I did or
I am doing or
Something I will do
Because I always wanted
To be an astronomer
Student, handicapped woman
And the mafia
Have nothing on me
Because I am just an astronomer
Just an astronomer

TWIST IT AROUND

My ship
That was supposed to come in
Was the Titanic
With all of the hoopla
The champaign
The smiles
The clothing
But when the chips were down
That's exactly where
My ship went
With all of my dreams
Hopes
Aspirations
I'm looking at a
Deaf woman
Thinking how lucky
She is
Not to hear my shit
I need to work out more
I need to starve myself more
I need to purge myself more
I need a plane
To take me out of my slump
I need to start all over again
I need to start all over again
At a younger age
I need to be 25
In the eighties
And I'm floating in space again
Watching my favorite bands performing
Please watch your language
Please watch your language
Please watch your language
It's very impolite
And I don't want
Anni Leibovitz
Taking a photograph of me
Unless she loses

All of the eighties stars
Who sold me on
All those bright ideas of wealth
And that it would never end
Like they had it in for my age
And when slackers came up like thistles
They could point the finger at me
And say that I caused the eighties
Seemingly to forget that they were the ones
Who put all of their money
In the years
And their clothing
And their hair
Another foul ball
Another foul ball
Another foul ball
Watch your language please
Turn it in on yourself
When it's a joke about me
You bitter bitch
Now that you've grinded your axe
In and on me
Does it make you happy?
Does it make you laugh when you think of me?
Does it make you
Want to give me prank calls
Not saying anything to me
Now I realized that
There never was a ship for me at all
Just a myth
That I could be myself
And not have to worry about
Getting burned
Before I forget
I must make my words clear as plastic
So everyone can understand them
So anyone won't be offended by them
So someone will like them
So someone will like them
So someone will like them?

.

FREEDOM FOR PLAY

Disturbing my straight piece
I need not a proxy
I am too busy
I hear all of the noises upstairs
And they disturb me
And I think when will my time come
To walk away in peace
But I worry that
This will be expurgated
The radio is playing too loud
And the door is not locked
Hard enough
As of today
Everything has gone missing
You only want something
When it's in plain view
And this puts me on a slow boil
Because you don't like
My career choice first and
Me second
And you wonder why
I'm constantly cutting my hair
And disconnecting my phone
Or leaving the machine on for days
Now I won't play by your rules
Because I don't like them
I've got a bottle of rage
And I'm going to open it
And let it explode onto you
My crime to you
Is what's between my legs
Even if it stays there
It's still a crime to you
But it doesn't matter to me anymore
I'm numb
And I've turned away
Because all of your sounds
Have just melted into

The noises upstairs

BOTTLED HOPE

I like to
Iron out
All of the rough patches
In the beginning
So there are none
In the middles
And with some luck
There won't be an end

BRAIN CHILDREN

Something to die for
So take me out to a golden field
Have a golden deaf woman
Fall in love with me
Heal me from this technology
Clean my brain
So I can feel
Preserve myself
But why bother for
I can't erase my tattoos
And I'll never meet
Beatrice Dalle
Or Leonard Cohen
Or Maurice Richard
Or anyone else
I admire or
Enjoy their dancings
Through this maze
Of programs that
Continue to drive me
Out of control
Nothing to die for
I have nothing
To die for
But a man who
Trained with dolphins
And who felt that
He didn't have to speak
I wish I was that man
I wish I was that man

GOING SOLO LAST

Do you have a ticket
For that seat?
I just had to write this down
That I wish
I could write like you
Write like that
Just the other day
And I am still breathing
She tasted like an apricot
Briefly
So sweet and soft
It's nothing
I had an idea
But it's nothing
I had a goal
And then
It's nothing
The last time
She was breathing
I wasn't
I don't want to breathe anymore
I don't want to
"Just had to write this down"
Anymore
I don't want to wish anymore
I want something to happen
All that happens
Is someone
Making sure that
I have a ticket
For my seat
I went by myself
Because she was
The last to kiss me

This piece was written on
friday august 25th at 4:00pm, 1995
in edmonton, ab

LONGEST PASSPORT PHOTO

Press a button
And the flash goes off
No sense of security
And the prospect
Of a safe home
Is not so warm
A man like that
Destroys you
And destroys me
A man like that
Shouldn't be a doctor
And I shouldn't talk
About her crisis
It all runs through me
With no sense of humour
And stains on my hands from the chemicals
From last night
All of this makes me
Feel alone
As I press a button

STREET CLEANER

I never knew
That titles were supposed to
Mean something
I thought the insides
Were the most important
Don't ask me
What it means
Make up your own meaning
Don't ask me
What it means
If what it means to me
Is most important to you
Then I pity you
Clear your mind for your self
And find what it means to you
Picture this
The goal tender is a long way away
Both teams are even
And one team is firing shots
On the invisible goaltender
What does it mean to me
Should mean nothing to you
Make your own mind
I don't need a title
That's why my titles are hollow
All I need are insides
And meaningful things to me
Meaningful things
That I never knew
Meaningful things
That you'll never know
Meaningful things
That don't need to be mailed in
Meaningful things
That I need to hold onto

JENNITA & JENNANNA

Jennita is 9
Jennanna is 11
And they are best friends
And are from Bosnia
And they walk into my work
And they have been deaf
From birth
And they know no language
But the one that they have created for themselves
And they have been in Canada
For a month
And everything is different
For now they can hear
Because they now wear hearing aids
So they hear
Sights
And they see
Sounds
That they haven't experienced before
And they haven't seen
Automatic water taps and doors before
This is all new to them
And I show them around my work
And they see a few
More wonders
And I wish I had money
And maybe I could help them more
But I use my camera
And I see their eyes
Light up with wonder and joy
As I hear their story
And see it copied in their young
Old faces
And I realize that
I have no reason
To register my disgust
With my present life
After hearing about

The wars they have seen
And I only know them
For three days
And they leave me
Wishing it had been longer
And they leave me
Missing their faces
And their brilliant way
Of communicating
The new found joys in their lives
And they leave me
Wishing I had more to give

written sometime in May of 1996 in edmonton, ab

NO JURIES, NO PRIZES

I can't help
But to feel
That your compliment
For me
Was bribed
Out of you
By me
Does this fit
With this title?
Should I re-arrange
All of this
So it justifies
Your hands
On the steering wheel?
Would it
Make you feel better
If I ate
My own skin?
Should I eat
My own skin?
I had
A winning number
But I lost it
So wipe that behavior
Right off of your face
I know full well
I need to be
Put in my place
Does that seem fair?
Does it kill you to create
Like it kills me
To create?
Like it kills me
To hear you
Tip toe
Around me
It kills me
And my creations

Kill me

WITHOUT HESITATION, ACCEPT IT OR REFUSE

Should I stick you in my hat
As I would a feather
I ask you this for I know not
How to do this
How to do it
Without sticking myself
In the eye
In my eye
It's taken me days to work this question
Into a form that seems more responsible
But even now
I feel it needs some kind of adjustment
So without hesitation
You accept or refuse
My question and myself
With all of my hesitations and indiosyncrocies

I look in my diary
For the date that I first met your eyes
And discover that this has no form or rhythm
So I need your answer to capitalize
How on earth I didn't die
In some fountain
That should have brought me life
I can't explain all of people's feathers
Because I have never had any
So how can I know something
I have never known in my eyes
I need these eyes to eleviate the pain
Of doubt in the fountain in your eyes
So this is why I speak my question
With the urgency of a terminal inmate
Of whispering truths and shouting lies

So now you know why
I don't make sense
I am having to

Clean this quickly off of my shelves
Before the virus grows
Hoping that you shine
To all that I wish to know

WILL YOU WILL

If I died unexpectedly
And I left you
A bottle of wine
A jacket
And a watch
What would you do?

Would you
Drink the wine quickly
With reckless abandon and no regard
As to how it would
Affect you?
Or would you drink it slowly
And savor the flavor
The smell and
The after taste?
Or would you save the bottle
Leave it unopened
And let it age
Picking it off of the shelf
To handle it
Thinking of the times
We once had
As your fingers
Caressed the bottle?
Whether you drink it or not
Would you
Make sure that no dust
Rests on the bottle
After it has been placed on its shelf?
Or would you
Give it up
By kindly depositing it
In the hands of a
Pass beggar?
What would you do?

Would you

Hang the jacket
In a closet
So as you
Only think of me
When you opened the closet door
Never wearing the jacket
Just looking at it
And touching it
When your mood would
Let you do so?
Or would you
Wear the jacket
With pride
In what we shared
In the past?
Would you
Wear the jacket
Whenever you went
Out in public
Whether you
Needed it or not?
Or would you
Just wear it
When you had to
With a slight grudge
Because the weather
Made you do it?
Whether you wore the jacket
Or not
Would it
Warm you to your soul?
Or leave a bitter taste
In your mouth?
What would you do?

Would you
Wear the watch
And count the
Hours, minutes, seconds
That have passed
Since you last
Spoke with me

Saw me
Touched me?
If you wore the watch
Would it remind you
Of times we once had
Times when I was
Very much alive?
Or would it
Just remind you
Of my shallow grave?
If you wore the watch
Would it be
Too tight?
Too loose?
Or just right?
Or would the fit
Even matter to you,
If you didn't wear it,
Would you still use it?
Or just leave it
On a shelf
With the bottle of wine
Or would it
End up
In the pocket
Of the jacket
In a closet?
Or would
All three of these items
Be used
At different times
In different places
For different reasons?
Or would they
End up
In a box
In some corner
Of a musty attic?
Hidden away
So no emotions
Would be stirred?
Or would these trinkets

Of my life
Stir any emotions?
Or would my
Untimely departure
Stir any emotions?

If I died unexpectantly
And left you
A bottle of wine,
A jacket
And a watch
What would you do?
If I died unexpectantly
And left you
What would you do?

Good morning
Good afternoon
Good evening
Or whenever you read this
Hear this
Or hopefully feel this
I have but one life to live
And I give it to myself
And on occasion
To others as well
I am whole now
For all of my pieces
Have fallen together
So that I have to remove
My dusty glasses
From my token face
And begin my broken write
So while I am in
This dull state
Let's pretend
For the sake of just pretending
That I am of some importance to you
This would give me more
To go for in a day
And let me wake for something
I have to pretend
For you only see me
And you don't know me
And it seems
That you don't want
To know me
But you have all heard
This before from me
All about my unintentionally
Reclusive life
So I will close this page
Finally, hopefully
With a great deal of pleasure
And turn a new page
One which is about

Some sort of epiphany
Which comes to compliment my
Somewhat used and roughed up puzzle
Which would be a
Departure from this solitary life
So
Good morning
Good afternoon
Good evening
Or whenever you hopefully
Feel this

WAKING MOMENTS

Feathers are only worth much
If the canary escapes the coal mine
I am bursting at the seams
With how much I need to create
I have got to paint
I have got to write
I have got to take pictures
I have got to
So much
That I often wonder
If that's normal
And if everyone feels this way
Most time I don't mind
If this is normal or not
And just do all that I do
And try to forget my moments
Of weakness and/or self doubt
So I can move forward
Instead of spinning my wheels
The canary has escaped
The coal mine and its captors
And has flown off into the sunset

CATCH UP

It's not my job
I keep on thinking about
And dwelling on my death
Hanging from stereo cable
Devastated by a head on car crash
Gun shot to my head
Strangled to death
Swallowing paint thinner
Getting hit by a bus
Overdosing on my medication
Terminal cancer
When one thinks like this
One fears nothing
Suicide
Murder
Naturally
Fear nothing
Show any doubt
And they will
Jump all over you
It's not my job
It's a career choice

You repulse me
You offend me
I need more
Than your bitter
Catch phrases
And stereotypes
To hold me down

Now
You have to show me it
Admit it
You wanted to
But I got wise
And changed my mind
And left again
On my own

I turn the lights out
Before I enter
Your room
So as I do not
Frighten and/or alarm
You
In your room

MASH

Why do I always
Fall in love
With attractive women
Who give me
The respect
I feel I deserve
When
The attractive women
Aren't finding me attractive?

It's only every second day
That I can even try
To forget about you
To try, really try and
Not to think about you
Usually
It doesn't work so well
Because I see you everywhere
Even though
You don't see me at all

I put your book
In a different place
Everytime I wake up
It keeps me on my toes

SOFT PROFILE

In an effort
To forget my past
I forgot how
To dream about
A future
So many obstacles
So little help
So many obstacles
So few friends
I try to make the best
Of any opportunity
No matter how small
I will not write
Anything out for you
Because you were
Part of my past
And had nothing
To do with my future
I came here alone
And will leave on my own
I always come here alone
And always leave on my own
No juries
No prizes
Just piss
Or get off the pot
You're not helping me
In either department
Remember
It's not about selling
It's about doing
At the beginning
I took my sight
Off of my future
And it fell upon
The obstacles
If you won't help
Then make like

An ice cube
On a scorching asphalt highway
On a scorching day
And melt away
To nothing

My flag
For some reason
Is always hung
At half mast
Because
Most times
I don't show
How proud I am
Of my family
Most times

If something was
Less than what I wanted
But more than
I could expect
I would accept it
Graciously
As if a pan handler
Would accept
A fifty dollar bill

I love the feel
Of a tight unprepared canvas
Underneath my hand
I could run my hand
Across it as much as
A lover's body
And get the exact
Same emotions

How hard do I have
To want you
Before you notice me
And then I die

BITCH

So,
So she said to me
That she would not
Carry a flag for me
It sounded as if
She said it over the phone

But I am almost certain
She said it in person
It's just that I wasn't
Looking at her
Because I knew
Somewhere inside
That she never cared
For me
And I didn't want her
To see my crushed face
My face reflected
My insides
So?

DISTURBING THE PEACE

As a child
And well into my teens
I was insulted and
Beaten on a regular basis
I was told to
Turn the other cheek
After years of this
Train of thought
I had turned the other cheek
So much
That both cheeks
Were bloody and worn through
Until my teeth were showing
My father told me
That sometimes you have to
Fight back
So I did
And the beatings stopped
And the insults were few

As a child
And well into my teen years
I only wanted
To mind my own business
So I did
But others continually
Badgered me
Helping me mind my own business
When I never need any help
Late in my teen years
I became hardened and
My views became extreme
And I decided
That when someone
Fucked with me
I would return the favor
And fuck with them
The nosiness dwindled

And I came to peace with myself

As a teenager
And well into my twenties
I accepted the indifference towards me
As I would all compliments
I grew into myself and
Grew out of hair and into tattoos
But others continually
Badgered me
I was told to
Turn the other cheek
Again
And again, it was just like
I was a child
I realized that some people
Never grow up
They are just like children
I will not turn the other cheek
Fuck with me and
I will fuck with you

As a child
And well into my teen years
As a teenager
And well into my twenties
This is what I learned and
This is what I practice
I mind myself
But
Disrespect me for no reason
And I will return the favor
I mind myself
But
Fuck with me for no reason
And I will return the favor
I am a product of your abuse
I am a product of your society
I am a mirror of your abuse
I am a mirror of your society
This is how I am
And I am at peace with myself

MEAN PRODUCTION

I am a product of your discrimination
I am a reflection of your hatred
You try to feed it to me
And I spit it back in your face
I don't like you
I don't expect you to care but
The next time you turn your back
Is the last negative action you make
For I will turn everyone against you
And cause you to die
Slowly and painfully
I am a product of your hatred
And a reflection of all of the
Negativity that you try to feed me
I will enforce the death penalty on you
With pride and no regret or remorse
Remember
Your discrimination, hatred and negativity
You carry
With pride and no regret or remorse
Remember
I am a reflection of your ignorance
Remember
I am a product of your ignorance
And you will never treat anyone like that again
For I will carry out the death penalty on you
And all the people that you stepped on
Will thank me
Under their breath

BAD HOUSES

If you can't
Laugh at your self
Then you can't
Laugh with or at anybody else
Fuck you and your altruistic ways
You never helped me once
Because I cared only for my work
And the gratification of the
Completion of my work
I won't go away
I will show your words of
Spite, jealousy and insecurity
To the world
And I will use your small words
Against you
You will see the error of your ways
The hard way
The best way for your bitterness
Lately
I can't stop myself
I tell myself I will not call
Even as I dial your number
After you answer
All I do is laugh
Laugh at you
Because you can't
Laugh with or at anybody else

MISANDRY

I am going through a cold snap
And I will not get out alive
I got a new pen
And I will pen myself a future
Now I want you to come to me
So I can tell you to go away
Now I want to gain wealth
So I can pay everyone off
And then disappear
For I am tired of playing
These run after you games
I don't remember being loved
I remember dreaming of being loved
Just last night I dreamt
That I was loved
And then left lost
By the one who loved me
And who I loved
I bought you flowers
And you just thanked me
And walked away
Never to be heard again
Never be heard again
Never heard again
Never heard
Never heard

I kept your quote
From last week's newspaper
To remind me
Of how narrow minded
Your type can be
Of how narrow minded
Any type can be

I had a dream last night
It disturbed me so much
I won't ever write about it

Happiness for me
Is about as rare as
A lesbian without an attitude problem

CRACKER BLUES

I remember when you
Drove me from your home
Just like it was
Fifteen minutes of fame ago
It's dirt
What I see
It's hurt
What I feel

I got this phone call
Late last December
With a probable tomorrow
That you didn't remember
I try
Not to care
But I'm
In its snare

I guess I ask too much
To tremble from your sight
To feel a whisper of your touch
Instead it's a whisper of your flight
How forced
Is this
How green
Is this

I will not be defined
By my immature write
I will not be labeled
By my downtrodden sight

Tooth for a tooth
Eye for an eye
I guess it's the time
I have to say goodbye

Drop you a line

When you didn't drop mine
You're just too busy
To spend me some time

It's dirt
What I feel
I try
In it's snare
How forced
Is this

Can anyone bare?

My credit is never good
When I try to rhyme
My credit is overpowering
When I reason

Proven justice
Depends on who's justice
And who is proven guilty

A PIECE OF THE SUN

Today was warm and sunny out
Just like the past few days
And on one of the past few
Beautiful days
I thought about sunflowers
And how they'll be in bloom
And how I feel that they are
The most happy flowers of all
Sunflowers are so happy
That they can offer you their seed
For food
I thought of taking a photograph
Of a fair haired and fair skinned woman
With a sunflower
Something about the combination
Seems so perfectly blissful
So perfectly content and happy
Although any woman with a sunflower
Would be a good combination
I would take the photograph
And keep it with me
When it is cold, cloudy, snowy, rainy
You get the idea
And it would remind me
Of warm and sunny beautiful days

EXPLORE YOURSELF

Explore yourself
Love yourself
Hate yourself
Masturbate
Mutilate
Eat, drink and be merry
Puke, shit and be depressed
Know yourself
Be unknown to yourself
Fantasize
Dream
Have nightmares
Go to bed early
Stay up late
Make friends with yourself
Make enemies with yourself
Be content with yourself
Never be content with your self
Bathe
Don't bathe
Do lots of drugs
Be straight edge
Explore yourself
I have
Have you?

I found out what my balls are for
And I discovered that they are very useful
They are for getting kicked time and time again

MASH NOTE

Would you be jealous
Of how much time I spend
With my work?
Or would you forget about me
Soon after we last talked?
Would you feel guilty
If I said you embarrassed me?
Or would it not phase you?
Would you feel guilty
If I said I embarrassed me?
Or would it make you embarrassed
To know that
I have been having
A mid-life crisis
For the last ten years?
Or would you just walk on by
Knowing I am just inches
From the hair on the back of your neck?
Would you remember my name
Even if I wasn't as intelligent
As the last person you met?
Would you be so kind
As to call me after I asked you to?
Or would you file my number away
And hide it away for good luck?
Would you accept my tastes
Or would you disrespect me
For my quickness?
Would you stop me from eating too much
Or would you let me get fatter and fatter?
Would you support me in my clean body
Or would you speak to me
Like I was a walking contradiction
Because of my tattoos?
Would you be and do
All of my requests?
Or would you say I ask too much?
Or would you say

I ask not enough?
For I have one more question
And I hope
It fits into your busy schedule
Would you be my bride?

I take Rohypnol
Everytime I work
On my art

She's laid out on Main Street
Put on display with her
Weak words
And weak videos
People are throwing
Pennies now instead of praise

SILLY QUESTIONS

Are my words rusty
Are my negatives over exposed
Are my brush strokes dusty
Is my work too much
Or still not enough
I decide all of the above
You judge all of the above
And I will ignore all of your misguided judgements
And continue on my path
Whether its rusty dust is too much
Until I am satisfied
That your vanity
Has been broken down
By my work

I want to be big enough
That you can't ignore me
But that I can ignore you

FAT UGLY BUTCH DYKE

I write this underneath
The harshest light
I have in my home

Five years ago
You gave me your number
And told me to call you
I did
Three times in six weeks
Leaving my number in each message
And still nothing
That was five years ago
And still nothing
I saw you last night
You used to be just an ignorant dyke
Well,
Now you've gained a lot of weight
And now you're an ignorant <u>fat</u> dyke
With a cute girlfriend
I don't know what she sees in your fat ass
I guess love really is blind

So when you walked by me
I looked you straight in the eyes
Daring you to greet me
You looked away sheepishly
Because you damn well knew better
Because you damn well knew
That I would have gouged out your eyes
With my house keys
You make me want to listen to Slayer
Non stop
At the highest volume possible for my current stereo
You make me want to take a hatchet
And hack my left hand off
And beat you senseless with my left hand
And then put the hatchet
In your sternum

Or maybe your throat

I have written this underneath
The harshest light
In my home
And I don't feel guilty about any of it

I don't feel guilty about one word of it
Not one word

HEY GIRL, STRANGE BOY

Hey girl
Strange boy
Whenever I go into this used book store
Hey girl
Hey cute young girl
Goes into the back
Until I have left
One day she had to serve me
Because her co-workers weren't around
She never looked me in the eye
I felt like I shouldn't be there
And to this day
I haven't went in again
I see her from time to time
And wonder what I did wrong
To hey girl
Makes me insecure
To strange boy

Don't believe in the Devil
Don't believe in Satan, Lucifer
Whatever
But I am going to make a deal
With the first devil that comes my way
If "it" exists

FEELING GUILT OR CONTEMPT

And when the war is over
And God is no more
And we aren't judgmental
Insecure raggles
We will volunteer our time
To different colours
To different differences
And we will be able
To look up from the sidewalk
That we are walking on
And look each other
In the eye
Without feeling guilt
Or contempt
For one self
And one another